AF484301

The Pretty Girls
Coterie of Poems

Vishakha Choudhary

BookLeaf Publishing

India | USA | UK

Dedicated to my sisters,

Nidhi and Jeewal.

Acknowledgements

Thank you

To all the people who have admired what I've penned in my life, thank you for your encouragement. I've steadily come this far because of those words.

To my family, thank you for standing by me.

To the Universe, I bow down in gratitude.

Preface

To all the women in the world who dream big, let your imagination be the limit of your wishes.

The Pretty Girls Coterie of Poems is your faithful accompaniment in times you wish to rant, vent and lose comportment. This quirky, satirical anthology is aimed at eliciting a laugh and a smirk, in that order. In the forty-one poems that belong to this collection, I hope you can find one relevant for occasions you might accidentally find yourself in. In case it fails to deliver, the author humbly apologises for the inconvenience. After all, it's your world!

Pick Your Mayhem

Dying Pretty

Oh no, did you hear?
The Duke's wife had an affair,
Gifted diamonds and secret alleys,
Not a secret her face belies.

Hush you, of no discernment,
Lest she rise of resentment,
To speak true of the dead,
Though I knew she was bad.

A mockery of station, and pedigree,
All know of her shopping sprees,
Loud mouth, a doll of botox,
No one could defeat that fox.

Gossip, champagne, a bunch of flies,
Tittering at the coffin that lies,
Of climbing classes and stolen gains,
Yes, the Duchess was a pain.

Garb of black, her visage white,
Loud in death, silent in life,
A sly sorceress, a cunning wife,
Oh beauty, the wielder of knife.

The Tailor of Husbands

A man I once held dear,
A mirage for him to be near,
Took him to the tailor by the shore,
And ours was a story worthy of lore.

His teeth a little crooked, his nose slant,
Alcohol his vice, too long his rant,
A touch too lazy, full of judgement,
The list long, an extra payment.

Zip and whirr, worked the tailor,
Unfazed and stoic, was his demeanour,
Curious about where he was stitched,
His eyes a river, a plan to be pitched.

My love, he had not much of cloth,
Looks or virtue, never both,
Cheaper to rather have him pretty,
The morals would cost a sack too many.

Pretty be a penny, good be a husband,
Rather have peace, than a misbrand,
Ode to the tailor for sewing fast,
Short the love affair did last.

Alice is Missing

Alice, O Alice,
Where did you go?
Was the world of wonder,
Too magical to let go?

Tea parties, garden viewings, puffs and creams,
Delicate steps, a tight corset, a perfect role,
Craving an adventure beyond dreams,
Did you climb down the rabbit hole?

The lure of a queen and a glorious battle,
Outshining a fiancé and his cattle,
To pick a sword than flatten dough,
Was our world ever enough?

Of mad hatters, Cheshire cats and fair queens,
Of vanity, judgement and silent screams,
Perhaps the scale was always titled,
Even a wise pupa would have wilted.

You outgrew a box and a chore,
Exploring the world and some more,
Letting go of glory and poise,
Seems like you finally made a choice.

The Tarot of the Secret Lane

You are right on track,
Prophecy of the tarot reader's deck,
Have self-love or your face may crack,
And we turn no payments back.

You've the queen in the cards,
Maybe you're nurturing at heart,
Oh, see here comes the king,
Your abundance is about to start.

Don't be sad, little doe,
It's destiny's game, not your woe,
The last time you stubbed your toe,
Well, that's for you to know.

You look for a relief,
Which plays hide and seek,
Only if you had more belief,
The cards would offer a peak.

You believe in the divine,
And the divine believes in you,
When you work hard and smart,
It will come true.

90° N

I am running to the North Pole,
With a book, matchsticks and a tattered sole,
Wait! Can't leave behind my winter clothes,
No wonder I've been called a slow poke.

All things electric, I will leave behind,
A dream in wilderness I would find,
Enough judgement for one life,
Perhaps I will find Santa and his wife.

Sad will be my loved ones,
Happier will be I,
Great is all the love,
Elusive to the eye.

Will you join my friend?
Leaving behind existence and trend?
Not able to make a single reel,
I wonder how you will feel.

Fret not, the snow doesn't judge,
Or polar bears for that matter,
The happiness that you don't fudge,
It will silence all the chatter.

Fall from Grace

Once it was unseen magic,
The other time no heir,
Heroines that are born to be tragic,
When was the world ever fair?

One time it was picking a sword,
Second the refusal to bow down,
Have they ever taken your word?
Too fast, please slow down.

Some tears shed at the birth,
More when you leave the house,
What is it to be a woman,
Is it all for a spouse?

Beware before your surrender,
They only like women of wonder,
Top to the bottom, head to toe,
Are you missing a dear foe?

Yin and yang, bread and wine,
We have the power to make it fine,
It's together we all rise,
My eyes search for that sunrise.

Hiding on Prom Night

Look at me,
What do you see?
No, don't tell me I'm pretty,
Listen, and you'll let me be.

In me I see,
A world of possibilities,
Playing the game to win,
I adore my responsibilities.

I choose to select,
Than wait to be chosen,
Picking my dress and my throne,
Not a doll from Frozen.

They ask, 'Hey babe,
Who's your plus one'?
My heart sings,
What about no one.

Whips of conjecture,
Moths of attention,
Rather go for a manicure,
And follow my passion.

The Lament of Medusa

I fear no trident,
Or an arrow in the quiver,
A fury so cold,
The snakes but shiver.

What is lost,
Can never churn gain,
The Olympus lies empty,
Deaf to my pain.

Eternal is a curse,
For the crime of another,
The prayers, the altar, the cries,
Why did I bother?

Broken, but unbent,
A stone to their light,
The betrayer will repent,
Mercy on their plight.

Never will I put,
Another on pedestal,
Join me sister,
Carve sorrow to festival.

Top of the World

One step, two steps,
A path did uncover,
A key to sunshine,
Danced the happy fever.

The things I love,
Did not come easy,
Those who love me,
The right side of cheesy.

Joy was the destination,
Fame was the consequence,
Money was intentional,
I bow to no inheritance.

Fluffy cupcakes, beautiful dresses,
Warm hugs, lush tresses,
A smile that all adore,
The future, a magic store.

Down tumbled the cup,
Silencing the reverie,
And just for a second,
I was at the top of the world.

Out of My Way

I shoot for the gold,
And avert no eyes,
My words always bold,
I play for the skies.

No time to waste,
On empty pleasantries,
One life, no haste,
Ran away the sentries.

Too long I've kept,
Playing a tug of war,
My life is mine,
Please raise the bar.

My days reflect light,
Not a shadow of someone,
Patience is a virtue,
I can go for a better one.

I talk no walk,
The walk is mine,
Chipping at the box,
The lacquer was fine.

Don't Say Sorry

Don't say sorry,
Just to be polite,
An overload of extra nice,
You decide the precipice.

A win is a win,
A loss no better,
Don't say sorry,
The ceiling won't shatter.

The hyenas to please,
A sorry won't appease,
Too heavy a burden to bear,
Not your albatross to wear.

Don't say sorry,
You are your favourite flower,
Nothing lasts forever,
Step into your power.

A comma never meets the end,
Chin up and head high,
Don't say sorry,
It's time to own your story.

Crying on My Birthdays

At one it was ignorance,
Food triumphed in year two,
Year three was a plain distraction,
For the four, I was to and fro.

In year six, it was snatching a gift,
Seven a lost promise of magic,
Ten saw the times sift,
Year thirteen was plain tragic.

Fifteen placed me at the top of the herd,
Sixteen saw the horror of puberty,
Seventeen labelled me as a nerd,
At eighteen, I wished I was thirty.

Twenty was a sack of expectations,
Losing myself at two-two,
The next year bought a cheer,
Two-five made life dear.

Things felt late at thirty,
Wise I was at thirty-five,
Forty did me a little dirty,
I was naive at fifty-five.

Gossip at 3 am

The actor's wife died,
Read the post in the morning,
What a pity cried the world,
Are you invited in the evening?

He had a mistress,
Or two if you will believe,
They might come to the funeral,
Crocodile tears to grieve.

Pity the poor wife,
Sweet and fragile,
A lonely dove all her life,
Radiant was her smile.

The man has a sort of look,
Which charms and beguiles and lies,
No wonder he was a crook,
You can tell by the pretty flies.

A devoted husband,
Read the obituary,
The end of a cheater,
Shouted the headline.

Sneakers and Heels

Thank you for your service,
Reads the email,
Toes screaming in the heels,
She can't possibly fail.

She's given up her weekends,
Buried her social life,
Days by the clock,
Has she been a good wife?

Practical was her mantara,
Emotions for the weak,
Empty nights and emptier days,
What did she actually seek?

Grateful for the sorrow,
Revelling in the tears,
A far-forgotten clarity,
Has it always been near?

I remember that girl,
Running by the park,
Blue were her sneakers,
And bright her spark.

Ditch the Frog

I kiss no frogs,
Weaving my own fate,
The world's an oyster,
Prince Charming can wait.

Black may turn to white,
Audacity may shout stale,
Not accounting for the tide,
It's never too late.

The meal is mediocre,
Would rather drink water,
Thousand tongues and one ear,
Careful, they might smother.

Pouring gold into stone,
The cracks are expensive,
Not a sin to atone,
Why so apprehensive?

He said, she said, they said,
The mill keeps milling,
Settling for the unworthy,
The pearls keep falling.

Three Faced

In an undusted attic,
Lay a forgotten doll,
Her drapes, a little matted,
In her hands, an old scroll.

Divine is she,
A painter of her purpose,
Dally and the river of life flows,
Uninterrupted into the chasm.

Craft an alluring mask,
And the heart will beguile,
Fingers on the strings,
An order with a smile.

A painted silhouette,
Shines the mirror on the wall,
Pluck a singular charm,
Watch your enemies fall.

Praise on a pedestal,
Flattery too uncouth,
Vanquished in the draughts,
Sweet whispers in the mouth.

Not So Demure

Just like the scenery,
Said the fool,
Your gaze strikes vigour,
Lilies by the pool.

A tiptoe over a gait,
Your fallacies are womanly,
The most beautiful bait,
Even a gilded knife is comely.

Pure is the velvet,
Until it strings the neck,
A napkin in the ravine,
Do not expect a call back.

An opera of jesters,
Too quick to anger,
The effigies gleam fair,
Wrapped around your finger.

Pity the simpleton,
And his herd of shadows,
A wine of molten glass,
A feast for the crows.

A Serving of Confidence, Please

A cup of courage,
Two shots of self-love,
A dollop of pride,
The glass would serve.

Eyes that don't hide,
A mouth that rings certain,
A heart that holds true,
Standing ahead of the curtain.

Morals that do not bend,
To the whims of another,
A fire so bright,
No ember could smother.

Bearing that defines grace,
A life worth living,
Beyond protecting a mask and a face,
I can foot the billing.

This is not a hand-me-down,
Earning a seat at the table,
All may care and the world may frown,
I write my own fable.

Fabulous Pose & Runny Nose

Set out to conquer,
Glossy is the smile,
In love with the competition,
Some may call her senile.

The eras fade,
And so fade the stars,
Murky waters to wade,
Stale went the caviars.

No is the keyword,
Not a victim of persuasion,
She is her own admirer,
What even is validation?

Petty are the battles,
Fought and bought,
A plaque doesn't decide,
The depth of her thought.

Some may call her irrelevant,
A picture-perfect pose,
Pretty is all you see,
Once upon a runny nose.

The Society's Barometer

Beauty lies in the eyes.
Yet the body pays the price,
Colour, shape, a pore on the cheek,
Limitless is the caprice.

A touch of fat,
Routine of a squat,
Gold in the tubes,
Cackles an idle bot.

The cloth won't fit,
Buy a magnifying glass,
The pride of a stick,
There goes the class!

Chase or attract,
The game is one,
Stipulations in the market,
The contract is fun.

Looking for a pillar,
Touch the concrete,
Next time opening your mouth,
Please be more discreet.

Kismat

Three little women,
Untie spools of wool,
Restless fingers weave an omen,
A fool's pride or a winner's tool.

Leave it to fate,
And the waters will carry,
Reins of a parched state,
The fumes herald destiny.

Battles are won,
Cattle are brought,
A lioness is no pawn,
A delicate fawn is well sought.

The sun does not bend,
To the will of the skies,
A heart of courage can end,
The agony of the cries.

Presents of the unworthy,
The sirens did wallow,
Walk the path,
And the path will follow.

Sugar-coated

A knife wrapped in velvet,
Words dripping with honey,
Screeches of laughter,
The bards find it funny.

The grace of a swan,
Belies the shadow of a shrew,
Or so said the whispers,
It must be true.

Iron wrought in porcelain,
Tall were the shadows,
The last tryst happened,
Right by the meadows.

The dignity of the courteous,
The barbs of the polite,
Enough tomes of etiquette,
Could mellow the bite.

Delicate fingers brush the hamper,
Ancestors bequeath inheritance,
A vat of venom boiled,
Thousand vials of fragrance.

Catching Teardrops

Drip, drip, drip, drop,
Fell another teardrop,
A hall full of opinion,
They simply wouldn't stop.

In a coven of
Endless cacophonies,
Musicians struck a chord,
The heart was empty.

Lips weighed down,
The freight of a smile,
A snake bit the apple,
A gift for the extra mile.

The saline doesn't melt,
At the crinkle of coins,
At the drapes of history,
The might of audacity.

A lonely tear waits,
On the slope of misery,
More comrades rush,
A party of drudgery.

Glorious Leftover

A line to step over,
Push and pull the hand,
Maids with no ties,
A lonesome band.

Refusal that is costly,
Borrowed is the dignity,
Whispers that pour,
Oil to the piety.

A girl and her cats,
The picture is empty,
A dome full of cheers,
Pristine were the sentries.

High up in the clouds,
Imaginary is your worth,
A debt to be repaid,
The labour of birth.

Hands are either held,
Or sketched is a line,
The crowd shouts miserable,
The dove just does fine.

Toad and Caviar

A foot mat of silk,
A basin of glass,
Eyes that refuse to meet,
Yoke and an inkstone.

A leash and a throat,
The neck was pretty,
The fallacies of the mighty,
Mirror of the petty.

Tape to the waist,
Measure of the bones,
Beauty turned to waste,
Milk is the shadow.

A casket of diamonds,
Butterflies sewn in a dress,
Bath of milk and rose,
The dead don't impress.

Flowers fall in the spring,
Ground full of mud,
In a bubble of illusion,
A toad feeds on caviar.

DIY Fairytale

There's no carriage rushing,
Or knights to the rescue,
A world full of pumpkins,
Mundane is the choice hue.

Gone are the fairy godmothers,
Or mice that are saviours,
Light your own cauldron,
A handshake and favours,

Once upon a magical cove,
A cafe on the side street,
An adventure beyond dreams,
Purchase the next ticket.

No ties that bind,
Loyalty is earned,
The last bird flying to the sun,
Vices that burn.

To wait is to waste,
To waste is to sin,
A paradise of sinners,
The mockingbird sings.

P for Productive

Did the skies ever
Drop a blessing?
The box looks down,
On the art of hustling.

Delicacies don't fall,
Into an open mouth,
Rigid waists and stationary minds,
Threads of the uncouth.

Moving a finger,
Creakes a joint,
If all do linger,
Rotten is the point.

Work is hard,
Intention of the smart,
Grave of the lazy,
Please do start.

A rise and rise story,
The poets will spin,
Rabbits fall asleep,
And the turtles win.

Queen of Frost

She is full of ego,
Chimes another she,
Look at her face and you'll know,
Cackled the bees.

Stone is the heart,
Saying no to a yes,
Unflinching doesn't match,
The tune of suppress.

A crown of morals,
Rests on a mind so quiet,
Joys of the simple,
Melt at the sight.

A lady self-assured,
Oh! The horror of the town,
The edges quite prickle,
The noses of the clowns.

Turn around and round,
Needles every centimetre,
A block of ice,
A hand raises the temperature.

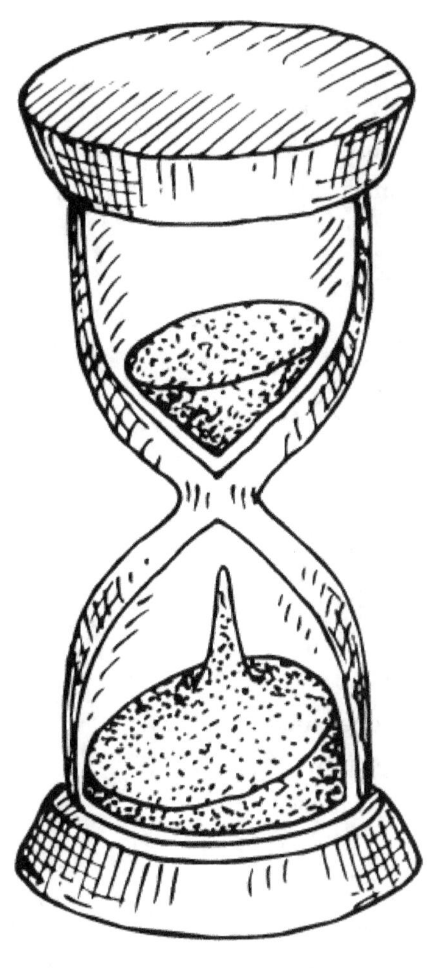

Clock said No

Clock said no,
My energy is mine,
Do not cross the line,
It's my time to shine.

Clock said no,
To worthless pursuits,
To wardrobes of suits,
I cut my own fruits.

Clock said no,
To ten thousand voices,
Chairs in offices,
I invite no bosses.

Clock said no,
To extra long rants,
Ill-fitting pants,
I choose my brands.

Clock said no,
To every forced yes,
Unwanted distress,
I am my own empress.

Sleep Says Goodbye

How do you do,
Owl of the night?
Many an unfinished battle,
Left to fight.

Dark are the circles,
Parched for relief,
Factory of the skull,
Defies all belief.

Trials and fires, hit and miss,
Longing for a would-be kiss,
Toss and turn, wide and narrow,
What is bliss?

Forget the eight,
Dreams are a gift,
The cogs turn perpetual,
And the sands sift.

Elusive and out of reach,
Sleep is a lover,
It's the fortunate who find,
A four-leaf clover.

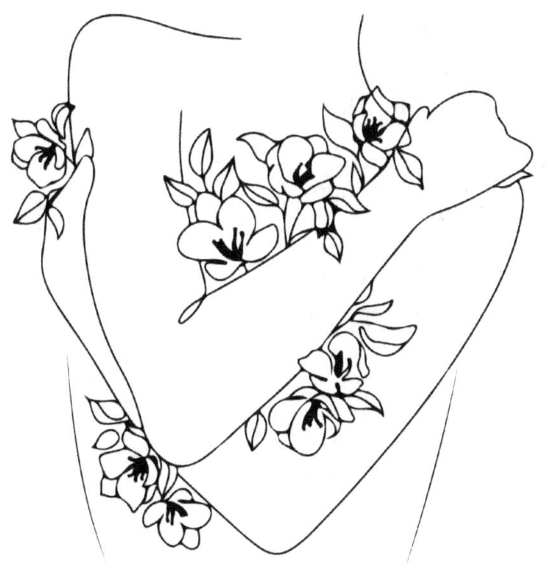

Graduating Life

Endings look magical,
Untied laces at the start,
This and that the world may say,
March to the beat of the heart.

Rainy days are inviting,
Learn to dance in the showers,
For love is not freely granted,
Starved are the leftovers.

The most beautiful dress
Can lie idle in a store,
If frowns become every day,
There's no bigger chore.

No rainbows in the sky,
Bring a box of colours,
A nightingale refuses to cry,
Sat down the beavers.

One portion is enough,
Lest the plate go stale,
Happy beginnings are wanted,
Scarce goes the tale.

Love Thy Pimple

A small pimple sits
In a garden with friends,
Angry is the gardener,
The destroyer of fiends.

Good things come in packages,
Bad ones never alone,
An uninvited guest knocks,
In search of a clone.

Traces to mend,
The tubes are empty,
Promise of a promise,
The shirt is frumpy.

It's ever the same,
Says the mirror on the wall,
A bearer to blame,
Available is the next stall.

Cold are the hands,
The fire still tall,
Dreams that are too big,
For a heart so small.

Glittering Venom

Half a head of hair,
Chapped is the lip,
So pretty is the lair,
A calculated fib.

A bear in hibernation,
Decades of woes,
Still is the fallacy,
Went away the foes.

An unkempt garden hides,
The beauty of a rose,
The catalogue is heavy,
Strike a new pose.

A hundred elixirs cannot,
Reverse a frown,
If dumpsters are dear,
Why vie for the crown?

To do or not to do,
Dear are the options,
A beetle called Pride,
Is up for auction.

Midnight Coffee

In a pink cup,
The middle of night,
Swims some espresso,
The aroma just right.

There's magic in the air,
At the hour of the witch,
A camera roll floats,
And the creative buds twitch.

Allure of the imaginary,
Stings of the real,
The kitchen counter watches,
All shades of feel.

A sigh and a breath,
The bag weighs away,
For precious few moments,
Lullabies sing and play.

Sugary are the lips,
A half-eaten toast,
A hidden cove of wonder,
Cocoa beans to roast.

Bye Bye, Cinderella

Girls would love
A fairy godmother,
With a good ear,
Sans will to smother.

The evil stepmother,
Distance will forgive,
Laments of the past,
Put into perspective.

A slipper of glass,
Too uncomfortable to last,
Sweep the broken pieces,
A search too fast.

The clock struck twelve,
Down went the marriage,
Perhaps the next time,
Buy your own carriage.

Bye bye, Cinderella,
Merry be your voyage,
Leaving behind the castle,
A destiny to forage.

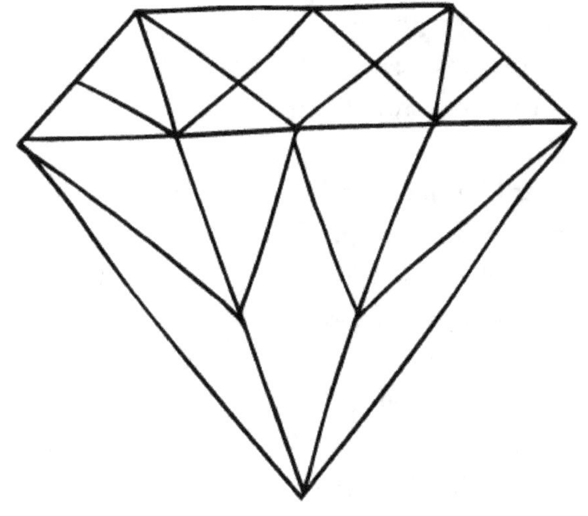

Pink Diamond

Remaining is the satchel,
A girl too reverent,
The pink diamond rests,
An inheritance to be spent.

First is the glassmaker,
The finest in the town,
Three loaves he offers,
An opera to crown.

Next is the metalworker,
With eyes very keen,
A bag of silver she offers,
For the sparkle and the sheen.

Last is the jeweller,
Troublesome to find,
A cart of gold on offer,
Royal ties that bind.

Who are you?
Whispers the breeze,
In the gloss of the diamond,
A girl holds a sneeze.

Flattery Accepted

Blush on the high,
Courtesy says happenstance,
It's a long, long journey,
The quest for acceptance.

Too shy and polite,
Hold your compliment,
Eyes that lose shine,
Carries on the merriment.

A stage too vast,
Stand in the centre,
Appeal of the corner,
Lost in the banter.

Laurels rest on the head,
Not hide at the feet,
Ignorant is the world,
Bring your own sheet.

Forgot the heels?
The carpet was red.
Fumes of jasmine,
Letters on the bed.

Blame the Mirror

Three white hair,
Flowing in a sea of black,
Beauty is a hidden rouge,
Sequestered in a precious pack.

Then appear the blemishes,
And the slight wrinkle,
A full stop or a comma,
A smile with a crinkle.

The most beautiful years,
Need not be temporary,
Head high and eyes alight,
Finesse a unique sanctuary.

Magnificent is the twilight,
A dance of the moon,
In the light of a fragrance,
Did the flowers swoon.

Every time a ballerina,
Led a troupe,
Eyes watched rapt,
Unaware of the coup.

The Perks of Audacity

Asking for sympathy,
And then forgiveness,
Keep your apologies,
Ran another governess.

If stairs to the moon,
Is the next dream,
Collect some bricks,
Cat with the cream.

All the tags,
Can fly in the dustbin,
Wasted wish-lists,
A cardinal sin.

Dream, then achieve,
Beseeches a lone peony,
The stars do believe,
Carving their trajectory.

For horses that are wild,
Reins to be steady,
The best time is now,
Better be ready.

Rejecting Rejection

Sorry for your loss,
Losing individuality is difficult,
Better luck next time,
Stretching the same cult.

An existence that thrives,
Beyond screens of statistic,
The rats can race,
The bees simply pick.

A stamp of approval,
Chasing a milestone,
The dogs are hungry,
Throw another bone.

Poor of the heart,
Counting blessings by number,
Self-worth is a knight,
That does not surrender.

Souls cannot weigh,
On the scales of mortals,
A trophy falls,
Shimmering glass of pedestals.

A Girl's Recipe

Looking for a cookbook?
It doesn't exist,
The divine of feminine,
Rule, war and persist.

Some soft fingers,
Crumpled a few empires,
Tittering and rumours,
Best left to squires.

A heart that nurtures,
Can easily swing the blade,
Jacks all around,
Few masters of the trade.

Skirt and a pant,
Narrow is the box,
Equals don't whisper,
'Oh! The sly fox'!

Rules are the same,
The packaging anew,
Wolves keep howling,
The queens continue.

Copyright @ Vishakha Choudhary
All Rights Reserved.

This book has been self-published with all reasonable efforts taken to make the material error-free by the author. No part of this book shall be used, reproduced in any manner whatsoever without written permission from the author, except in the case of brief quotations embodied in critical articles and reviews.

The Author of this book is solely responsible and liable for its content including but not limited to the views, representations, descriptions, statements, information, opinions, and references ["Content"]. The Content of this book shall not constitute or be construed or deemed to reflect the opinion or expression of the Publisher or Editor. Neither the Publisher nor Editor endorse or approve the Content of this book or guarantee the reliability, accuracy, or completeness of the Content published herein and do not make any representations or warranties of any kind, express or implied, including but not limited to the implied warranties of merchantability, fitness for a particular purpose.

The Publisher and Editor shall not be liable whatsoever...

Made with ❤ on the BookLeaf Publishing Platform

www.bookleafpub.in

www.bookleafpub.com

www.ingramcontent.com/pod-product-compliance
Lightning Source LLC
Chambersburg PA
CBHW061700130726
47996CB00006B/2099